Contents

Celebrating spring 4

St David's Day 6

St Patrick's Day 7

Purim 8

Holi 10

Mother's Day 12

Ramnavami 13

Id-ul-Adha 14

April Fool's Day 16

Pesach 17

Easter 20

Baisakhi 24

Al-hijrah 26

St George's Day 27

Wesak 28

Glossary 30

Index 32

Words printed in **bold letters like these** are explained in the Glossary.

Celebrating spring

After the cold of winter, spring is a joyful time. The weather gets warmer and the days get longer. Nature seems to come back to life. The trees burst into bud and the first flowers bloom. It is a time of new life and celebration.

Many festivals are held in springtime. Some mark the end of winter and welcome in the spring. Many have special religious meanings, when people remember the birthdays of their gods or teachers and important times in their religion's history.

Many baby animals are born in spring.

Festivals are often happy times with many ways of celebrating. There are special services and ceremonies, delicious food, dancing, cards and gifts. Some festivals are holidays when you have a day off school.

Some festivals happen on the same day each year. Others change from year to year. For festivals that change, you will find a dates circle, which tells you when the festival will be. (The future dates of some festivals are only decided upon nearer the time, so some dates in the circles may be out by a day or two.)

Dates

7 April 1998
26 April 1999
15 April 2000
4 April 2001
8 April 2002

Moon dates

The calendar we use every day has a year of 365 days, divided into 12 months. Most months have 30 or 31 days. Some religions use different calendars which are based on the Moon. A Moon month is the time it takes for the Moon to travel around the Earth. This is about 27 days, which gives a shorter year. So, each year, the Moon calendar falls out of step with the everyday calendar. This is why some festivals fall on different days each year.

St David's Day

On 1 March, Welsh people celebrate St David's Day. St David is the **patron saint** of Wales. According to legend, he was a **Christian monk** who lived hundreds of years ago. He was famous for his **holy** powers. When his teacher went blind, David gave him back his sight.

St David lived with his monks in a **monastery**. It was a very hard life. The monks were not allowed to speak and had only bread, salt and vegetables to eat. David later became **archbishop** of Wales.

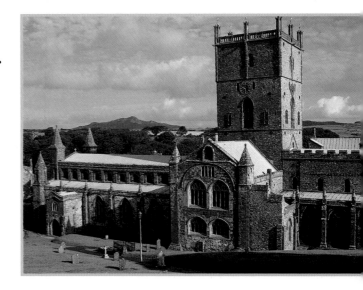

St David's **Cathedral** in Wales.

Leeks and daffodils

To celebrate St David's Day, people wear leeks or daffodils pinned to their clothes. The leek is a sign that winter is over. The daffodil is a sign of spring.

St Patrick's Day

On 17 March, Irish people celebrate St Patrick's Day. St Patrick is the **patron saint** of Ireland. This is a very jolly day and no one goes to school or work. There are parades through the streets and lots of parties.

Patrick was born in Britain hundreds of years ago. When he was just 16, he was **kidnapped** and taken to Ireland to be sold as a slave. He later escaped and became a **priest**. St Patrick spent his life teaching people about **Christianity**.

These girls are dancing in a St Patrick's Day parade in Dublin.

Three leaves

On St Patrick's Day, people wear a three-leaved shamrock. St Patrick is said to have used the three leaves to teach people three ways of thinking about God.

Purim

The **Jewish** festival of Purim is held in February or March. It remembers the **Jews** who lived in Persia more than 2000 years ago. A man called Haman helped the king to rule. He hated the Jews and wanted to have them all killed. The king agreed. But when he realized that his wife, Queen Esther, was Jewish too, the king gave orders for Haman to be killed instead.

A play for Purim

Purim is a very joyful festival. Children go to fancy dress parties and play tricks on their parents. They also put on plays and act out the story of Purim. You could try doing this with your friends.

At Purim, many Jews go to the **synagogue** to hear the story of Queen Esther. Every time wicked Haman is mentioned, children try to make as much noise as possible. They boo, shout, stamp their feet and shake special rattles, called greggors. All this is done to drown out the sound of Haman's name.

Dates

12 March 1998
2 March 1999
20 March 2000
9 March 2001
26 February 2002

Special three-cornered cakes are eaten at Purim. They are called Hamantaschen, or sometimes Haman's purses. They are made of pastry filled with honey and poppy seeds.

Holi

Holi is the happiest festival in the **Hindu** year. It is celebrated in February or March. It marks the end of winter and the coming of spring. In India, where Holi began, this was when farmers celebrated the first harvest of the year.

It is best to wear your oldest clothes for Holi. You may get covered with brightly coloured water or powder!

On the night before Holi, a big bonfire is built. This reminds people of the wicked witch, Holika, who gave the festival its name. There was once a prince who worshipped the god, **Vishnu**. Holika tried to kill him by burning him in a fire. But Vishnu saw what was happening and rescued the prince from the flames.

Next day, the real fun begins. People play tricks and squirt each other with coloured water. These are like the games that the god, **Krishna**, used to play with his friends. In the evening, people visit their relations with gifts of sweets and wish them happy Holi.

Roasting coconuts

In some places, people throw coconuts into the bonfire as offerings to the gods. They leave them to roast, then break them open and eat the sweet insides. They believe that this gives them the gods' blessings.

Mother's Day

The six weeks before Easter are called Lent. This is a very serious time for **Christians**. They remember the time **Jesus** spent in the desert, **fasting** and thinking about how to do God's work.

Dates

22 March 1998
14 March 1999
9 April 2000
25 March 2001
10 March 2002

Mothering Sunday, or Mother's Day, falls on the fourth Sunday in Lent. On Mother's Day, children give gifts of cards and flowers to their mother to thank her for all the good things she does throughout the year.

Mother's Day service in church.

Happy Mother's Day!

Try making your own Mother's Day card. Decorate it with flowers made of card or twists of tissue paper. Stick them on with glue or tiny pieces of double-sided tape. Then write a poem inside.

Ramnavami

Dates

5 April 1998
25 March 1999
12 April 2000
2 April 2001
Later dates not known

At Ramnavami in March or April, **Hindus** celebrate the birthday of the god **Rama**. Rama is one of the most popular of all the Hindu gods. He is the hero of the Ramayana, a very long poem which is one of the Hindu **holy** books. It tells the story of Rama and his beautiful wife, Sita, who is **kidnapped** by Ravana, an evil demon king. With the help of the monkey god, Hanuman, Rama finds Sita and rescues her.

On Rama's birthday, Hindus go to the **mandir** to hear the Ramayana being read. They also sing songs of worship and take turns in rocking a cradle with an **image** or picture of Rama inside.

Rama and Sita with their friend, Hanuman the monkey god.

13

Id-ul-Adha

Id-ul-Adha is a **Muslim** festival, held at the end of the **Hajj pilgrimage**. This is a special journey to **Makkah** which all Muslims hope to make. Makkah is a city in Saudi Arabia. It is the Muslims' most important **holy** place, because it is where the **Prophet Muhammad (pbuh)** first taught people to follow **Allah**.

Dates
7 April 1998
27 March 1999
15 March 2000
7 March 2001
25 February 2002

These Muslims are on the Hajj pilgrimage to Makkah.

Id-ul-Adha is celebrated all over the world. It is the time when Muslims remember the story of **Ibrahim** from the Qur'an, their holy book. Ibrahim was about to kill his son to show how much he loved Allah. Just in time, a voice told him to stop. He killed a goat instead.

Today, at Id-ul-Adha, Muslims kill a sheep or lamb to remind them of Ibrahim's love for Allah. Butchers do this for Muslims in Britain. Some meat is given to friends and relations. Some is given to the poor. People also give each other gifts and cards, and wear new clothes.

Muslims visit the **mosque** for prayers at Id-ul-Adha.

Five Pillars

The Hajj is one of the Five Pillars of **Islam**. These are five duties Muslims try to carry out:
1 Believing in Allah and Muhammad (pbuh).
2 Praying five times a day.
3 Giving money to the poor.
4 **Fasting** during the holy month of Ramadan.
5 Making the Hajj pilgrimage to Makkah.

April Fool's Day

On 1 April it is April Fool's Day, a time for playing tricks and practical jokes on your family and friends. You could hide their shoes, or pretend someone wants them on the phone.

Anyone who falls for a trick is called an April Fool. It is great fun thinking up new tricks to play. But watch out! If you don't play your trick by midday, you become the Fool instead. And make sure the tricks you play are not dangerous!

No one knows why 1 April was picked for this festival. It might be that now spring has come, everyone wants to have some fun.

April Fool!

Hunting the Gowk

In Scotland, April Fool's Day is known as Hunt the Gowk. A gowk is a cuckoo or a fool. A trick is called a huntegowk. It must be played before midday or you become the cuckoo.

Pesach (1)

The **Jewish** festival of Pesach celebrates how God helped the **Jews** escape from Egypt long ago. Their lives were very miserable. They had to work like slaves. A man called **Moses** was chosen by God to lead the Jews to safety. But the king of Egypt sent his army after them. There seemed no way of escape. But God parted the waters of the sea so that the Jews could cross. Then the water flooded back, drowning the Egyptian soldiers.

The parting of the waters.

Pesach (2)

At Pesach, **Jews** celebrate with a special meal called the **Seder**. As they eat, they tell the story of the first Pesach. The youngest child in the family asks four questions. The first is 'Why is this night different from all other nights?' The other questions are about the food on the table. Each dish has a special meaning.

A Jewish family sitting
down for their Seder meal.

Pesach is a serious festival when Jews remember their history. But it is also a happy time for being with your family. Pesach is also called Passover.

Special foods

At the Seder meal, Jews eat bitter foods, like **horseradish**, *to remind them of how unhappy the Jews were in Egypt. They also eat sweet foods to celebrate their freedom. There is a dish of flat, dry crackers called matzot. The Jews left Egypt in such a hurry, they could not wait for the bread they were baking to rise. Eating matzot reminds them of this.*

Charoset (a sweet mixture of apples, nuts and wine) – for the cement used by Jews in buildings for their Egyptian masters.

Horseradish – has a bitter taste for unhappiness.

Parsley – a sign of spring and of hope.

A dish of *salty water* stands for tears.

Lamb bone – for the lambs killed in Egypt and offered to God.

Hard-boiled egg – another offering to God.

Easter

For **Christians**, Easter is a special spring festival. It is when they remember how **Jesus** died on the cross and celebrate how he came back to life again. The story of Easter is told in the Bible, the Christians' **holy** book.

This **church** window shows Jesus on the cross. This is called the Crucifixion.

Jesus went to **Jerusalem** for the Passover (or Pesach) festival. He knew that his life was in danger because his enemies did not like what he taught. He shared a last meal with his followers and then went to a garden to pray. While he was there, soldiers came for him. He was put to death by being nailed to a large wooden cross. Two days later, when his friends visited his tomb, they found it was empty. Jesus had come back to life! They saw him several more times before he went up to heaven.

Jesus's coming back to life is called the Resurrection. Christians believe it shows that death is not something to be afraid of. It is the start of a new life with God.

The cross

There are crosses in every Christian church. Some Christians wear a cross as a necklace or a badge. The cross reminds them of how Jesus died. This is why people eat hot cross buns at Easter.

Holy Week

The week before Easter is called **Holy** Week. It was the last week of **Jesus**'s life. It begins with Palm Sunday, when Jesus rode into **Jerusalem** on the back of a donkey. Crowds of people came to cheer, waving palm leaves to welcome him. When **Christians** go to **church** on Palm Sunday, they are given a small palm-leaf cross to remind them of that day.

(Note: In the Orthodox Church, Easter is celebrated on different dates.)

Easter service in church.

Jesus died on Friday. The name Good Friday comes from 'God's Friday'. It also refers to Jesus's goodness, because Jesus was good to give up his life for others. He rose from the dead on Easter Sunday. This is a very happy day. Christians attend special services in church to thank God for Jesus's life.

Easter eggs

Do you know why people give chocolate eggs at Easter? Eggs stand for new life. They celebrate Jesus's rising from the dead. Eggs also remind us of spring, when many animals have their young.

Decorating eggs

You could try decorating your own eggs for Easter. First empty an egg by making two holes with a pin, one large and one small, in each end of the egg. Blow through the small hole so the egg comes out of the big hole at the other end into a bowl. Wash and dry the egg. Then you can paint your egg, or cover it with pieces of tissue paper glued in place, or even give it a face and add woollen hair.

Baisakhi

On 14 April, **Sikhs** celebrate the festival of Baisakhi. This is the start of the Sikh New Year and an important day in Sikh history.

On Baisakhi in 1699, the Sikh leader, **Guru Gobind Singh**, called all the Sikhs together. He asked if any of them would die for their beliefs. Five men stepped forward. But the **Guru** did not kill them. His question was a test. Instead, they became the first members of a special group called the **Khalsa**.

At Baisakhi the special flag which flies outside the **Gurdwara** is taken down and a new one put up in its place.

Today, Sikhs celebrate Baisakhi with services in the Gurdwara. These may last all day. There are readings from the Sikhs' **holy** book, the Guru Granth Sahib, and a special meal to share. This is also the time when many young Sikhs join the Khalsa. Then they count as full members of their religion.

The Five Ks

When Sikhs join the Khalsa, they promise to wear five signs of their beliefs. These are called the five Ks.

1 *Kesh – uncut hair. Sikh men wear a **turban** to keep their long hair tidy.*
2 *Kangha – a comb to look after your hair.*
3 *Kara – a steel bracelet.*
4 *Kirpan – originally a sword, but now often small enough to be worn on the comb under the turban.*
5 *Kaccha – cotton shorts, now usually worn under clothes.*

Al-hijrah

Dates

27 April 1998
16 April 1999
5 April 2000
26 March 2001
15 March 2002

Al-hijrah is New Year's Day in the **Muslim** calendar. It is the day on which Muslims remember the **hijrah**, a journey which the **Prophet Muhammad (pbuh)** made hundreds of years ago. Muhammad's teachings about **Allah** were unpopular in **Makkah**, where he lived. So he moved to another city, called Madinah. Here many people became his followers.

Al-hijrah means the day of the hijrah. Muslims celebrate by telling stories about Muhammad and saying extra prayers.

This is the Prophet's **Mosque** in Madinah, the city in which Muhammad settled.

Muslim calendar

The hijrah is so important for Muslims that they start their calendar from the date on which it happened. After each year, Muslims write the letters AH which mean 'year of the hijrah'. The year 1999 is 1420 AH.

St George's Day

St George's Day is on 23 April. St George is the **patron saint** of England. Legend says that he was a soldier who lived hundreds of years ago. He was famous for his bravery.

Once George met a fearsome, fire-breathing dragon. It had already eaten several children from a nearby town and was about to gobble up the king's daughter. George killed the dragon and rescued the young princess. In return, the townspeople became **Christians**, like George.

On St George's Day, many people wear a red rose. This is the special flower of England.

St George's **emblem** was a red cross on a white background. It decorated his armour and shield. It is now used as part of the English flag.

St George killing the dragon.

Wesak

The **Buddhist** festival of Wesak happens in April or May. On this day, many Buddhists celebrate three special events: the **Buddha**'s birthday, his enlightenment, and his passing away (death). Enlightenment means suddenly seeing things clearly. It is a bit like turning on the light in a dark room. It means that the Buddha saw the truth about the world. It is this truth that he taught his followers.

A **monk** talking to Buddhist children on Wesak Day.

Wesak is the biggest Buddhist festival. It is also called Buddha Day. Buddhists decorate their homes with lamps and flowers and send Wesak cards to their friends. Then they dress in simple, white clothes and visit the **vihara** to pay their respects to the Buddha. It is a day for being especially kind and generous to others, as the Buddha taught.

Dates

9 May 1998
30 April 1999
18 May 2000
7 May 2001
Later dates not known

Jataka stories

At Wesak, children listen to stories about the Buddha. These are called Jataka stories. The Buddha often appears as an animal in the stories to teach an important lesson. In one story, he is a lion whose life is saved by a jackal. Instead of eating the jackal, as a hungry lion would, he lets him go. This teaches the children that one good turn deserves another.

Glossary

Allah – Muslim word for God

archbishop – very senior Christian priest

Buddha – great teacher who lived about 2500 years ago

Buddhist – someone who follows the teachings of the Buddha

cathedral – important Christian church, where a bishop (senior priest) is based

Christian – person who follows the teachings of Jesus

Christianity – religion of the Christians

church – Christian place of worship

emblem – special symbol or badge

fasting – not eating or drinking

Gurdwara – Sikh place of worship

Guru – Sikh teacher

Guru Gobind Singh – Sikh leader who started the Khalsa

Hajj – pilgrimage made by Muslims to Makkah

hijrah – journey which the Prophet Muhammad (pbuh) made from Makkah to Madinah. It marks the start of the Muslim calendar.

Hindu – to do with the Hindu religion which began in India about 4500 years ago. A Hindu is someone who follows the Hindu religion.

holy – means respected because it is to do with God

horseradish – bitter-tasting plant root, used to make sauce

Ibrahim – prophet of Islam who was ready to kill his son to prove his love for Allah

image – picture or statue of a god or goddess

Islam – religion of the Muslims. It began about 1400 years ago in Saudi Arabia.

Jerusalem – city in Israel which is very important for Jews, Christians and Muslims

Jesus – religious teacher who lived about 2000 years ago. Christians believe that he was the son of God.

Jewish – to do with the Jewish religion

Jew – person who follows the Jewish religion, which began in the Middle East more than 4000 years ago

Khalsa – the Sikh community, or family. A special ceremony is held for Sikhs joining the Khalsa.

kidnapped – taken away against your will

Krishna – popular Hindu god, often shown with blue skin. Krishna is famous for playing tricks.

Makkah – city in the country we now call Saudi Arabia where the Prophet Muhammad (pbuh) was born. It is the Muslims' holiest place.

mandir – Hindu place of worship. Also called a temple.

monastery – place where monks live and worship

monk – man who gives up his possessions and devotes his life to God. Monks have to obey a strict set of rules.

Moses – great Jewish leader who lived about 3500 years ago

mosque – Muslim place of worship

Muhammad – the last great prophet of Islam. He was chosen by Allah to teach people how to live.

Muslim – person who follows the religion of Islam

patron saint – saint who looks after a particular country or a particular group of people, such as travellers or doctors

pbuh – these letters stand for 'peace be upon him'. Muslims add these words after Muhammad's name and the names of the other prophets.

pilgrimage – special journey made to a holy place

priest – holy man or religious leader

prophet – person chosen by God to be his messenger

Rama – popular Hindu god

Ramadan – holy month for Muslims when they fast from dawn to sunset every day

Seder – special meal eaten at the Jewish festival of Pesach

Sikh – person who follows the Sikh religion, which began in India about 500 years ago

synagogue – Jewish place of worship

turban – long piece of cloth which Sikh men wind around their heads to keep their hair tidy

vihara – Buddhist place of worship

Vishnu – one of the most important Hindu gods. Vishnu is worshipped as the protector of the world.

Index

Al-hijrah 26
Allah 14, 15, 26, 30
April Fool's Day 16
archbishops 6, 30
Baisakhi 24–25
Bible 20
Britain 7
Buddha 28, 29, 30
Buddhists 28, 29, 30
cards 5, 12, 15, 29
Christianity 7, 30
Christians 6, 12, 20, 21, 22, 23, 27, 30
churches 20, 22, 30
Crucifixion 20, 21
Easter 20–23
Egypt 17, 19
England 27
fasting 12, 15, 30
food 5, 9, 11, 18, 19, 23
God 12, 17, 23
Good Friday 23
Gurdwaras 25, 30
Gurus 24, 30
Guru Gobind Singh 24, 30
Guru Granth Sahib 25
Hajj 14, 15, 30
Haman 8–9
Hanuman 13
Hindus 10, 13, 30
Holi 10–11
Holy Week 22–23
Ibrahim 15, 30
Id-ul-Adha 14–15
India 10
Ireland 7
Islam 15, 30
Jerusalem 20, 22, 30
Jesus 12, 20, 21, 22, 23, 30
Jews 8, 9, 17, 18, 19, 30
Khalsa 24, 25, 31

Krishna 11, 31
Lent 12
Makkah 14, 15, 26, 31
mandir 13, 31
monasteries 6, 31
monks 6, 28, 31
Moon months 5
Moses 17, 31
mosques 15, 31
Mother's Day 12
Muslim 14, 15, 26, 31
New Years 24, 26
Palm Sunday 22
Passover (see Pesach)
patron saints 6, 7, 27, 31
Pesach 17–20
pilgrimage 14, 15, 31
prayers 15, 26
priests 7, 31
Prophet Muhammad (pbuh) 14, 15, 26, 31
Purim 8–9
Qur'an 15
Rama 13, 31
Ramadan 15, 31
Ramayana 13
Ramnavami 13
St David's Day 6
St George's Day 27
St Patrick's Day 7
Saudi Arabia 14
Scotland 16
Seder 18–19, 31
Sikhs 24, 25, 31
Sita 13
synagogues 9
viharas 29, 31
Vishnu 11
Wales 6
Wesak 28–29

Contents

Charities and animals 4

Looking after animals 6

Stopping cruelty 8

Medical care 10

Animals helping people 12

Protecting animals 14

All at sea 16

The right environment 18

Farming 20

Education 22

The future 24

Raising money 26

How you can help 28

Glossary 29

Contact details 30

Index 32

Words printed in **bold** are explained in the glossary.

Do you have a pet? Lots of people do. As well as keeping animals as pets, we watch them on television, read stories about them and visit them in zoos. Animals are interesting. Animals are fun.

All through history, animals have been used for food, transport and to help people do their work.

Sadly though, some people hurt animals or don't care for them properly.

Some animals are at risk of dying out because they are hunted, or their **environment** has been damaged or destroyed.

There are more types of animals in rainforests than anywhere else in the world.

Some charities help protect animals from sickness and harm, and find them new homes where they are well cared for. Other charities work to save unspoilt areas like rainforests and jungles, so wild animals can live undisturbed.

Humans are animals.
Which animals are most like us?

♡ Looking after animals

Caring for animals is not easy. Sometimes animals are hurt because people do not know how to look after them properly. Other times, animals are abandoned because people do not want to care for them any more.

CASE STUDY

Sasha the dog was found on the streets. Battersea Dogs Home, which takes in thousands of lost dogs and cats each year, found her a new home with 11-year-old Tim. 'Sasha is a very popular member of my family,' he says. 'She is ever so friendly and well-behaved.'

Bugs the rabbit was brought into the Blue Cross animal hospital after being attacked by a cat. After treatment, Bugs recovered and he now lives in a much safer hutch. Charities such as the Blue Cross teach people how best to care for their pets so that fewer animals are lost or mistreated.

Bugs is very happy now that he is properly cared for.

Find out how your friends look after their pets.

♥ Stopping cruelty

Animals feel pain - just like people.
Some people are cruel to animals and
do not treat them with the respect
and care they need.

The Royal Society for the Prevention of
Cruelty to Animals (RSPCA) is the only charity
to have trained inspectors. They can check
that animals are not being mistreated. Bad
owners are reported to the police and new
homes are found for the animals.

Why do you think people are cruel to animals? What can be done to stop them?

♥ Medical care

Have you been to the doctor's recently? Animals need to visit the vet sometimes, and it can cost a lot of money.

CASE STUDY

Max couldn't breathe properly when he got a ball stuck in his throat. He was rushed to a PDSA PetAid hospital where he had an operation to remove the ball. Max is now fit and well again.

Homeless people can get very lonely living on the streets, so many of them like to keep dogs as pets. But they cannot afford to take their dogs to the vet. The National Canine Defence League provides them with free health checks, **vaccinations**, **worming** and flea treatments.

What would you do if you found an injured animal?

♥ Animals helping people

If you have an animal living in your home, it's probably a pet. But animals can be very useful too. Around the world, many people keep animals to help them do their work.

In Ethiopia, people use donkeys to get around and help them carry things, instead of cars and tractors. The Donkey Sanctuary has clinics where the donkeys can be treated if they are hurt or sick.

The Donkey Sanctuary teaches people how to look after their donkeys so that they are stronger and able to work longer.

CASE STUDY

Endal, a dog trained by Canine Partners for Independence, has changed Allen Parton's life. Allen was badly injured when he was a sailor in the Gulf War in 1991. He has difficulty remembering things and has to use a wheelchair. Endal does lots of different things for Allen. He helps with the shopping and at the cash machine, and fills up the washing machine. 'Above all,' Allen says, 'Endal has taught me to love, laugh and live again.'

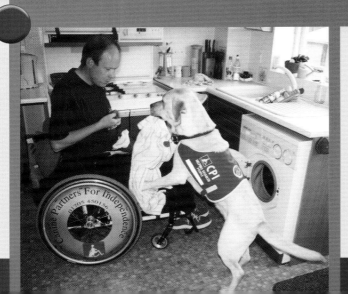

What other animals can you think of that help us?

♥ Protecting animals

We all need somewhere where we can live safely. Animals are the same. Sadly though, many animals are at risk of dying out because the places where they live have been damaged and their food has been destroyed. Other animals have been hunted.

Did you know that a rhino's horn can grow up to two metres long?

Since 1970, nearly all the rhinoceroses in the world (97 percent) have died out. This is because they have been hunted for their horns, and the places where they live have been taken over by people. Save the Rhino International has placed 18 black rhinos back in East Africa where they are protected from hunters.

Bill Jordan, a vet, set up Care for the Wild International to protect wild animals from harm. He has written books, made **governments** change their laws and advised people around the world how to best look after wild animals.

What other animals need protecting?

Animals in the sea are as much at risk as animals on land. The number of fish in the sea is going down as too many are being caught. And every day, five million items of rubbish are dumped into the sea, killing and hurting sea creatures.

In what other ways are our seas being damaged?

One hundred million sharks are killed each year – mainly for their fins that are used in cooking. The Marine **Conservation** Society has made sure that the basking shark – which lives in the seas around the UK – is now protected from fishermen.

CASE STUDY

Corky is an orca (also known as a killer whale) who lives in a marine park. She has had seven pregnancies, but none of her babies (known as calves) survived. WDCS, the Whale and Dolphin Conservation Society, helps orcas like Corky by campaigning to return them to the wild and to stop them being caught in the first place.

Orcas are members of the dolphin family and have never been known to kill a person in the wild.

Do you live in a hot country or a cold one? Animals generally prefer one or the other. Zebras like dry areas with open spaces. Some birds and water creatures prefer plant life that grows in wet, marshy land.

If animals are to live happily and **breed**, they need to live in the right place.

CASE STUDY

Bewick's swans return year after year to marshy land provided by the Wildfowl and Wetlands Trust (WWT). There used to be many more areas like this, but they have been drained of water so that houses and roads can be built on the land. The WWT land is one of the few places left in the UK where Bewick's swans can be found.

Many of the places wild animals like to live in have been destroyed to make space for farmland or housing. Charities help to protect areas from damage, so that animals can live safely.

In the 1970s, only 200 Golden Lion Tamarin monkeys were left in the wild. Most of the forest they lived in had been destroyed. WWF moved some of these monkeys to a new forest where they are safe. WWF is also planting more forests so there will be more room for the Golden Lion Tamarins, and there are now 1000 of them living in the wild.

♡ Farming

Hamburgers, sausages and roast lamb... most people today like to eat meat or other animal products like cheese, yogurt and butter.

However, many farmed animals do not have enough space to move around. They are not able to eat the food they like and have to travel long distances in crowded lorries.

CASE STUDY

Pregnant pigs on farms used to be kept in stalls, like these. They were too small for the pigs to turn around in. Compassion in World Farming managed to get the stalls banned in some parts of the world, so that **sows** now have more room and can get comfortable.

The RSPCA has teamed up with supermarkets to make sure that farm animals are cared for properly. Farmers that meet these standards have their food marked with the 'Freedom Food' label.

Think of other ways you can check that farm animals are well looked after.

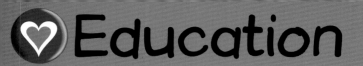

If you have a pet, you probably know how to care for it. If we are all to care for the animals in the world around us, we need to know more about them: how they live, what they eat, and what they need to survive.

CASE STUDY

Every year Wildlife Explorers, the junior section of the Royal Society for the Protection of Birds (RSPB), gets children to join in its Big Garden Birdwatch. Children learn more about birds by noting how many and what type of birds they have spotted in their gardens. Then the RSPB can work out which birds are doing well and which ones need more help.

How would you clean a cat's teeth? What should you do if you find a cat that's been hit by a car? Like many other charities, Cats' Protection has a website to help teach us the best ways to care for our pets.

Where else could you find out about caring for animals?

♥ The future

We live in a world where there are many thousands of different types of animals. But every year hundreds of **species** die out. Once gone, they will never come back again.

Zoos and animal charities around the world are working together to save species at risk.

CASE STUDY

The Zoological Society of London has helped save the Arabian oryx, a type of gazelle that lives in the desert of the Middle East. About 20 years ago the last wild oryx was killed. Oryx that had been living and breeding in zoos have now been let loose in the desert and are doing fine.

Some animals are so at risk in the wild that their only hope for the future is being bred successfully in zoos.

Raika, at London Zoo, is one of only 500 Sumatran tigers left in the world. They are hunted for their body parts. It is hoped that she will soon have cubs, to help increase the number of remaining tigers.

We all have a duty to look after and care for animals. Make sure you do.

♡ Raising money

Charities are able to help others because they are given money. This money is **donated** by governments, businesses and people like you and me. Together we raise millions of pounds for charity each year.

There are many fun ways to raise money for charity. It doesn't matter how silly or simple the idea is - as long as it helps.

Your class could paint and draw pictures of different animals and create a calendar to sell at Christmas.

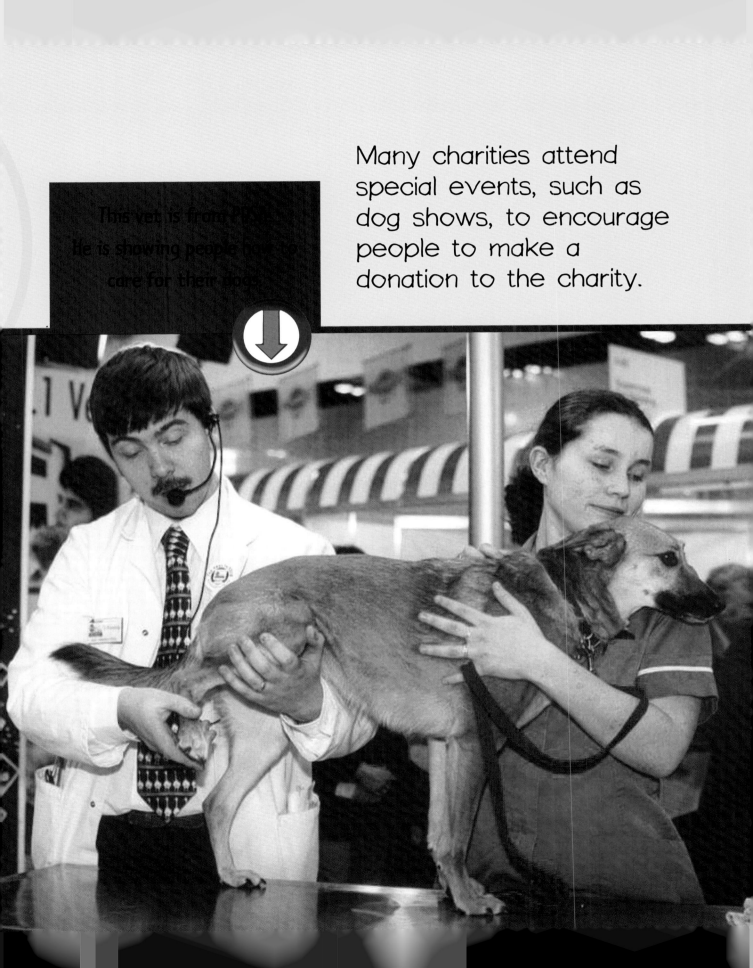

This vet is from PDSA.
He is showing people how to
care for their dogs.

Many charities attend
special events, such as
dog shows, to encourage
people to make a
donation to the charity.

♥ How you can help

If you care about animals, you can help by:

● contacting a charity that you are interested in (see pages 30-31) to find out more about what they do. Many charities have children's clubs that include competitions and games, as well as providing information.

● asking your teacher to get someone from an animal welfare charity to come and talk to your class.

● looking up (after getting permission from your parents or a teacher) one of the animal charity websites.

● getting your family to buy **organic** or **free range** foods or those with the Freedom Food symbol.

● not buying a pet animal unless you know you and your family will be able to take proper care of it throughout its life.

● raising some money for the animal charity of your choice on your own or through your school. Get your parent, carer or teacher to contact the charity to find out more.

Glossary

breed	to reproduce and have babies
conservation	work done to preserve something for the future
donate	to give
environment	the world around us, including the land, the air and the sea
free range	describes farmed animals that have space to move about
government	the people who make laws and rule the country
organic	a term to describe farmed animals and plants that have not been given artificial chemicals
sows	female pigs
species	a type (of plant, animal, bird or insect)
vaccinations	injections that animals have to protect them from disease
worming	when an animal is given drugs to kill parasites in its body

♥ Contact details

All the charities in this book do many more things to help animals than those described. Contact them to find out more.

Battersea Dogs Home
020 7622 3626
www.dogshome.org
info@dogshome.org

Blue Cross
01993 825500
www.bluecross.org.uk

Care for the Wild International
01306 627900
www.careforthewild.org.uk

Cats' Protection
08702 099099
www.cats.org.uk

Compassion in World Farming
01730 264208
www.ciwf.co.uk

The Dian Fossey Gorilla Fund
020 7483 2681
www.dianfossey.org

The Donkey Sanctuary
01395 578222
www.thedonkeysanctuary.org.uk

Marine Conservation Society
www.mcsuk.org
info@mcsuk.org

National Canine Defence League
020 7837 0006
www.ncdl.org.uk

PDSA
01952 290999
www.pdsa.org.uk

Royal Society for the Prevention of
Cruelty to Animals (RSPCA)
0870 333 5999
www.rspca.org.uk

Royal Society for the Protection of Birds
(RSPB)
www.rspb.org.uk/youth

Save the Rhino International
020 7357 7474
www.savetherhino.com

Whale and Dolphin Conservation Society
0870 870 5001
www.wdcs.org
info@wdcs.org

Wildfowl & Wetlands Trust
01453 891900
www.wwt.org.uk
slimbridge@wwt.org.uk

WWF-UK
01483 426444
www.wwf-uk.org

Zoological Society of London (London Zoo)
www.zsl.org

Organisations in Australia and New Zealand

Australian Animal Protection Society
www.aaps.org.au

RSPCA
(02) 6282 8300
www.rspca.org.au

Royal Guide Dog Association
(02) 9412 9300
www.guidedogs.com.au
info@guidedogs.com.au

♡ Index

animal hospitals 4, 7, 10, 12

birds 18, 22, 29
breeding 18, 24, 25, 29

cats 6, 7, 23
cruelty 8-9

dogs 6, 9, 10, 11, 13, 27
donkeys 4, 12

environment 5, 18-19, 29

farming 20-21, 29
fish 16
food 20, 21, 28

hunting 14, 25

marsh land 18
money 26-27, 28
monkeys 19

new homes 5, 6, 8, 9

orca 17

oryx 24

pets 4, 6, 7, 10, 11, 12, 22, 23, 28
pigs 20, 29

rabbit 7
rainforest 5
rhinoceroses 14, 26

sea animals 16-17
sharks 16
swans 18

tigers 25
transport 4, 12
treatment 4, 11, 12

vets 10, 11, 15, 27

websites 23, 28, 30-31
wild animals 5, 14, 15, 16, 19
working 4, 12-13

zoos 4, 24, 25